MEDITATIONS
ON THE
KINGDOM

Stephen Kaung

ISBN: 978-1-942521-53-2

Available from:

Christian Testimony Ministry
4424 Huguenot Road
Richmond, Virginia 23235

www.christiantestimonyministry.com

Printed in USA

CONTENTS

PREFACE

The messages contained in this booklet were given as spoken ministry by Brother Stephen Kaung during the spring and summer of 2005. The first four messages were given in Richmond, Virginia as a series of meditations on the Kingdom of God. The last message was given as part of a series of ministries given during the Western Christian Conference in Santa Barbara, California. It is included here because of its relevance to the earlier meditations given in Richmond. The messages have been transcribed and printed by permission with minimal editing for clarity.

SEEK YE FIRST
THE KINGDOM OF GOD

Matthew 6:33—But seek ye first the kingdom of God and his righteousness, and all these things shall be added unto you.

Shall we pray:

Dear Lord, as we gather together in Thy presence, our hearts do bow before Thee and say, "Lord, speak to us." Do not allow us to come to Thy presence and fail to hear Thy voice. In spite of all our weaknesses, Lord, we pray that Thou wilt come to us and give Thy Word to us, and by Thy Word give us strength that we may follow Thee. Our heart's desire is that Thou may really have us for Thyself because Thou art worthy. We commit this time into Thy hand and trust Thy Holy Spirit to take charge and to do Thy work. In Thy precious name we pray. Amen.

This morning I would like to do something different. This morning you are here not to hear me speak but to join with me in meditation. I want every one of you to participate in this meditation. We are going to meditate on this Word of God and allow the Spirit of God to really speak to our hearts.

Oftentimes we gather to hear a message and forget it afterwards. Meditation is very important. If we hear the Word of God but do not meditate, we lose it. Before we leave the meeting it is gone. The Bible tells us that we need to meditate on, to think over, to pray over, and really open our hearts to His Word, letting it sink deeply into our hearts and transform us. I think this is something the modern world has lost. This modern age has lost the art of meditation, and therefore the spiritual life of God's people is shallow, superficial, and unreal. Meditation deepens our spiritual life. So I would like you to join with me to meditate.

The Lord has drawn my heart to this one verse: "Seek ye first the kingdom of God and his righteousness, and all these things shall be added unto you." These words, spoken by our Lord Himself, are not only an exhortation, they are a command. He commands us to seek the kingdom of God and His righteousness first, and all these things shall be added unto us.

THESE THINGS

What are "all these things?" If you read the preceding verses, all these things are related to the things of this life, our biological life. All these things are the things of this world—what we should eat, what we should drink, what we should be clothed with. Eating, drinking, and clothing are the necessities of this life. We live in this world, so we need to eat, we need to drink, we need to be clothed with in order to live. Unfortunately, these things can become our priority. In other words, we seek these things first, and then if we have the time or energy, we will seek the kingdom of God. We reverse the priority that our Lord Jesus set for us. This is normal for the people of the world, because they do not have the heavenly Father. Therefore, they have to help themselves. They have to take care of their lives in order to live. They worry, they seek, they are careful about these things because nobody will take care of them. They have to take care of themselves—what they should eat, what they should drink, and what they should be clothed with. This is their life. This is what they live for. This is their purpose for living, nothing else. They are concerned about it; they are anxious about it; they seek for it; and they give their life to it. That is but right for the nations. Our Lord Jesus Himself said, "These are the things that the nations seek for."

A HEAVENLY PEOPLE

But who are we? We who believe in the Lord Jesus, we who have been born from above have been translated from the kingdom of this world into the kingdom of the Son of His love. In other words, our citizenship is in heaven. We are a heavenly people, but we live on this earth. We live, as it were, in two kingdoms. On the one hand, we live in the kingdom of God. How do we know? You remember that our Lord Jesus in His conversation with Nicodemus said, "Verily, verily I say unto you, unless you are born of water and of the Spirit, you cannot enter into the kingdom of God. He that is born of the Spirit is spirit."

So we have been born of the Spirit. We have been transferred from earth to heaven. We have a new life and are under a new rule. On the one hand, we belong to the kingdom of God. That is where our citizenship and our loyalty lie. Yet on the other hand, we are still on this earth. How should we live upon this earth as sons of the kingdom of heaven? I think this is a very practical problem. All of us are involved in this, and we have to find a way to live as a heavenly people on this earth. What should be our priority? How should we live? Should we live as the people of this world, seeking all these things—eating, drinking, clothing, and security for this life, laying up treasures on this earth in order to be sure that we have enough?

LOVE NOT THE WORLD

Our Lord Jesus used a parable about a rich man who had so much he did not know what to do with his plenty and said, "I know what to do. I will tear down my barns and build a bigger one and put all my corn into it. Then I will say to my soul, 'Soul, you do not need to worry anymore. You have plenty to eat.'" And our Lord Jesus said,

"Tonight I want your soul." What happens to all that you have hoarded? "Vanity of vanities! All is vanity."

The things of this world are temporary. What are the things of this world? In I John 2 it says, "Love not the world, nor the things in the world." The lust of the eye, the lust of the flesh, and the pride of life are the things that are passing away. And if we seek these things, if we put our time, our life, our energy, our all into seeking these things, remember that it is like pursuing after wind or trying to catch your shadow. They will soon pass away. That is why the wisest of men, Solomon, said, "Vanity of vanities! All is vanity." But you say, "We have to live. If we do not seek these things, they will not be dropped from heaven. Who will take care of us? We have to think of our security. We have to give our time to the world." We do not know that this is the strategy of the enemy.

When the children of Israel were in Egypt under hard labor, they cried to the Lord, and the Lord sent Moses to deliver them. But when Moses faced Pharaoh and said, "God said, 'Let my people go that they may serve Me,'" Pharaoh said, "These people have too much time to think about spiritual things, religious things. Increase their hard labor. Work them to death, so that they have no time to think about spiritual things. All their time will be occupied with their stomach. Their stomach will become their god and nothing else."

OUR PRIORITY

This strategy of the enemy has not changed. Look at God's people today. Where are they? How do they use their time? Where goes their energy and thoughts? What occupies their whole life? Especially as we are approaching the end of days, the pressure from the enemy will increase. And how should we live under such conditions? Are we satisfied with our Christian life? Where goes all our time? We have no time for the things of God. Our priority is wrong. Our Lord Jesus said that we who are the citizens of the kingdom of God should seek first the kingdom of God, and then all these things shall be added unto us. Do you believe it? Is it true?

The nations must take care of all these things. But our Lord Jesus said, "Your heavenly Father knows. Look at the birds of the air. Look at the lilies of the valley. How much more precious you are in the sight of God. Will He not take care of you if you first seek His kingdom and His righteousness?" What is the result if we seek these things of the world first and then, if we have time and energy, we seek the kingdom of God? If we live as the people of this world, all these things will never satisfy us. People seek all these things—eating, drinking, and clothing. The more you seek the more you want. You will never be satisfied. You will not be content with the things that you have, and at the same time, you will lose the kingdom. Is it worthwhile? Is it not time that we wake up?

What is our priority—the kingdom of God or the things of this world? Many times we are occupied with the things of this world. We consider them important. We consider them a "must." We must do them. This is something we have to do, but the things of God can be put aside. They are not that urgent, not that real. The things of this world are real. But brothers and sisters, what is real? Where are we? We are so occupied with the things of this world. We know much about the things of this world, but how much do we know about the kingdom of God? We are in the world, yes, but we are not of the world.

Think of Abraham. God called him out of this world. By faith he lived in the land of promise, but he lived in tents all his life. He was a stranger and a sojourner in this world. Are we strangers in this world? If we are strangers, then we will be sojourners.

Look at Lot. He lived in the world just like Abraham, but how differently he lived. He became a dweller in this world. He moved his tent toward Sodom and then lived in Sodom. Even though his righteous soul bothered him, yet he remained in Sodom. Even when the angels came to deliver him, he hesitated, and his wife looked back and became a pillar of salt. The Bible says, "Remember Lot's wife" (Luke 17:32). Do we remember?

How should we live on this earth? This is a practical question. I believe it affects every one of us. We need to live, to eat, to drink, to be clothed with, and to take care of our family. But what is the first thing to us? Let us answer this question before God. Think about it. Who is first? What is first? Is God first in our lives? Is the kingdom of God first in our seeking? Is it true? If this is the case then our Lord said, "All these things shall be added unto you."

THE MESSAGE OF CHRIST AND THE APOSTLES

When our Lord Jesus was on earth, what was His message? "Repent, for the kingdom of God has drawn nigh." Even after He was resurrected, during those forty days when He appeared to His disciples, what did He teach? He taught them about the things of the kingdom of God. What did the apostles proclaim? The apostles proclaimed the message of the kingdom of God. On the day of Pentecost, Peter stood up and said, "This Man Jesus whom you crucified, God has made Him Lord and Christ." It is the kingdom.

At the end of the book of Acts, during Paul's two years of imprisonment, he preached the kingdom of God and taught the things concerning our Lord Jesus. This is the message of the church. But today this message is lost. The best you can hear is the gospel of grace. Everything is grace, forgiveness of our sins, going to heaven. It is all grace, grace, grace. We do not even hear that there is a kingdom of God, and we are in that kingdom. We are not told of the things of that kingdom or how we should live in that kingdom. When the kingdom of God shall come upon this earth, where will we be? It is a lost message, and that is the reason God's people today are so weak spiritually. You are in the kingdom of God because you are born from above. But do you live in that kingdom?

What is kingdom? The very word *kingdom* in Greek, first of all, is an abstract noun. It means "sovereign rule, dominion, kingship." Second, it is a concrete noun. It means "people, population, territory over which the king rules." According to the Scriptural concept, *kingdom* is basically "kingship"; that is, the kingdom of God is nothing but God's own expression. The kingdom of God expresses God Himself. What a God He is! His own character characterizes His kingdom. Or to put it in another way, everyone who is in that kingdom, everyone who is under His rule,

13

everyone who obeys Him will be transformed and will take up the character of God, the King Himself. That is kingdom; that is the kingdom of God. All who are in the kingdom of God should be under the rulership of God, and if you are under the rulership of God, you will be changed. You will be transformed. You will take up the character of your King, thus proving that you are a true son of the kingdom.

Oftentimes we are afraid of the word "authority." But Paul said, "Authority is for building up, not for tearing down." The real purpose of God's authority is to build us up, because only when we submit ourselves under the authority, the kingship, the kingdom, and the rule of God will His authority then do the work of transforming and conforming us to the character of God. That is the only way. But in the most general sense, the kingdom of God is from eternity to eternity, because from eternity to eternity He is God. So everything is under His rule.

His kingdom is an everlasting kingdom, but unfortunately there were rebellions, not only in the heavenly hosts but also among men on earth. In other words, God's kingdom extends over all. It is the kingdom of all ages. His dominion is over all. Everything is under Him. That is the general meaning of the kingdom of God. Even Satan and rebellious men are not out of His control because His kingdom extends over all. But strictly speaking, the kingdom of God speaks of those who put themselves under His rulership, who obey Him, who allow Him to work the kingdom character into their lives. These people are really the sons of the kingdom of God. Now, are we there?

CHARACTERISTICS OF THE KINGDOM OF GOD

In order for us to live in the kingdom in reality, I think we need to understand what is the kingdom of God. Oftentimes we think of the kingdom of God in historical terms. In other words, one day the kingdom of God will come upon this earth. In the book of Revelation we find that one day the kingdom of this world will become the kingdom of our Lord and of His Christ. Thank God for that. It is coming. But it is more than historical. The kingdom of God is spiritual. In other words, it has already come, it is now here, and it will come. Unless we are really living in the kingdom of God today in reality, when the kingdom of God shall appear upon this earth, we will be shut out. The Bible says that we will be gnashing our teeth in darkness, repenting that we have lost our opportunity. It does not mean we lose our salvation. In eternity, yes, we will be there, but during the kingdom age we will not be there. It all depends upon whether we live in the kingdom of God today as an obedient citizen of the kingdom. We know much about this world, but how much do we know about the kingdom of God? What are the characteristics of the kingdom of God?

The Kingdom of God is Everlasting

First, the kingdom of God is everlasting and eternal. In Psalm 145:13 it says, "Thy kingdom is a kingdom of all ages, and thy dominion is throughout all generations."

In II Peter 1:11 it says, "For thus shall the entrance into the everlasting kingdom of our Lord and Saviour Jesus Christ be richly furnished unto you." Everything on this earth is temporary. No matter how precious things are, they will pass away. Only the kingdom of God is everlasting. So seek not the things that pass away. Seek the things that will remain forever. Everything that you possess in this world will pass away. You are not able to carry them with you. When people are buried, even when they bury their treasures with them, they cannot enjoy them. They are gone. Naked we come and naked we go, but that which is of the kingdom of God remains forever. Are we working for things temporary or are we really seeking for things eternal?

The Kingdom of God is Spiritual

The kingdom of God is spiritual. It is different from this world. Everything in this world is physical and earthly, but the kingdom of God is spiritual. In Romans 14:17 it says, "The kingdom of God is not eating and drinking, but righteousness, and peace, and joy in the Holy Spirit." It is different from the kingdom of this world. The marks of the kingdom of this world are eating and drinking because they have nothing more. That is all they have. But the kingdom of God is not eating and drinking; it is righteousness, peace, and joy in the Holy Spirit. In other words, the kingdom of God is spiritual. It is righteousness, what is right in the sight of God.

It is peace. What is peace? This world does not have peace, because the god of this world today is a murderer. There is no peace. Peace only comes from God. Our Lord Jesus said, "I give My peace to you; I leave My peace with you."

It is the joy of the Holy Spirit. If you look at this world, you may find people laughing, but that is pretense, not true. Joy is of the Holy Spirit. When the Spirit of God in you is joyful, you are happy, you are joyful. That is the joy in the Holy Spirit. Now do you have joy in the Holy Spirit? In other words, does the Holy Spirit rejoice in you because you listen to Him, you obey Him, you cooperate with Him? When you do that, that is joy unspeakable. That is real joy. Then you are in the kingdom of God.

Our righteousness must exceed the righteousness of the Pharisees and the scribes. They have righteousness but it is

external, in letter. Ours is within and of the Spirit. Do we have that? The kingdom of God is spiritual, and because it is spiritual it is always here. It is not limited by time or space. Today we must live in the kingdom of God by being righteous, at peace, and filled with the Spirit of joy.

The Kingdom of God is Internal

The kingdom of God is internal. It is not something outward. In Luke 17:20-21 it says that our Lord, having been asked by the Pharisees when the kingdom of God was coming, answered them saying, "The kingdom of God does not come with observation; nor shall they say, 'Lo here' or 'Lo there:' For behold, the kingdom of God is in the midst of you."

There are two different translations. One says, "The kingdom of God is in the midst of you." Christ was in their midst. He is the kingdom of God. If you have Christ, if you take up the character of Christ, you have the kingdom. Another translation says, "The kingdom of God is within you." It is not something external; it is something within you, in your spirit. Today, the kingdom of God cannot be observed by naked eyes. But it does not mean it is not there. It is there. Wherever Christ is, there is the kingdom of God. And the Christ in you and the Christ in me is the kingdom of God. It is internal.

The Kingdom of God is in Power

Then, as I Corinthians 4:20 says, "The kingdom of God is not in word but in power." In other words, it is not what you say but what you experience of the power of God in your life. You may know a lot about the teaching of the kingdom of God, but that is not the kingdom of God. That is only its teaching. The real kingdom of God is power—the power that transforms you, delivers you from this world, and overcomes this world. That is the kingdom of God.

The Kingdom of God is Love

Finally, the kingdom of God is love. God has translated us, transferred us out of the kingdom of darkness, the power of darkness, into the kingdom of the Son of His love (see Colossians 1:13). If we really are constrained by the love of Christ, we are in the kingdom.

THE REALITY OF THE KINGDOM

"Seek ye first the kingdom of God and His righteousness and all these things shall be added unto you." What should be our attitude and response to the kingdom of God? Do you say, "Well, it is too spiritual to be real. To me it is not real." It is because you live by your outward man and what you can see, hear, feel, and touch. The things of the world are real to you. The things of God are unreal. But if we live by the Christ-life in us, there is nothing more real than the kingdom of God.

"Seek ye first the kingdom of God." What is seeking? Seeking is not a casual word. Seeking involves purpose, determination, and energy. You set your heart upon it. That is seeking. Ask yourself if you are really seeking the kingdom of God. Have you *ever* sought the kingdom of God? Is that the purpose of your life? Are you determined to find it? Are you willing to pay any cost to get it? Are you willing not to stop until you find it? It is deliberate. It is with effort. Do you make it your priority? Or is your priority the things of this world? "What about me? What about my family? What about this and that?" Do you ever ask, "What about the kingdom of God?"

"Seek ye first the kingdom of God." If we really seek the kingdom of God, we will apply ourselves, we will make it our first priority, and we will be willing to sacrifice other things because this is more important to us. This is the word of our Lord, His advice to us. He says, "You are living in this world. All these things are necessary, but you should not live like the nations; you should live like My children."

GOD'S PROVISION

"Seek ye first the kingdom of God." If you do that, the Lord said, "I will take care of you." Thank God He never fails. By the grace of God I have served Him over seventy years. I can testify that His Word is true.

"Seek the kingdom of God and His righteousness, and all these things shall be added unto you." The reason we are so worried about all these things is because we put a wrong emphasis on life. Godliness with contentment is great gain. The Lord may not promise us luxuries, but He promises us our necessities. Isn't it wise if we seek the kingdom of God first? That should revolutionize our life.

PRAY FOR THE KINGDOM OF GOD

The Bible tells us that we should pray for the kingdom of God. In the so-called Lord's prayer, He teaches us to say, "Our Father, who art in heaven, hallowed be Thy name, Thy kingdom come."

What is prayer? Prayer expresses our heart's desire. Do we really desire the kingdom so much as to pray for it, that it may come, that it may come into our life and come into this world? Have you ever prayed, "Thy kingdom come"? What is our prayer? Do we pray, "Give me this, give me that. Hurry!" If it is too slow, we murmur. If it does not come, we are offended. Or do we pray, "Thy kingdom come"? Prayer should change our life. We think that prayer changes things. No, prayer changes you. If you pray, you will be changed.

Do you ever pray a kingdom prayer? Evan Roberts, the vessel used by God in the Welsh Revival, 1904-05, hid himself after the revival for a number of years. And when people asked him what he was doing, he said, "I am praying kingdom prayers."

PROCLAIM THE KINGDOM OF GOD

Proclaim the kingdom of God. "The glad tidings of the kingdom of heaven must be preached throughout the whole world as a testimony, and then the end will come" (Matthew 24:14). The kingdom message, the gospel of the kingdom must be preached throughout the nations to prepare the way, and then the end will come.

BE WORTHY OF THE KINGDOM OF GOD

And the Bible says, "Be worthy of the kingdom of God" (II Thessalonians 1:5). In everything we do—the way we spend our time, the way we set our priorities, the way we live, the things we are occupied with—we need to ask ourselves, "Am I worthy of the kingdom of God? Is this the way that the sons of the kingdom should live?" Brothers and sisters, let us meditate on this Word of God.

Shall we pray:

Dear Lord, Thou hast spoken to us, "Seek ye first the kingdom of God and his righteousness, and all these things shall be added unto you." We believe You. We believe Your Word. And now Lord, may Thy Spirit bring us into practicing Thy Word, that Thou may prove to us how faithful Thou art. Oh, deliver us from the things of this world. Enable us to live under Thy Kingship. We honor Thee. In Thy precious name we pray. Amen.

THE VIOLENT SEIZE THE KINGDOM

Matthew 11:12—But from the days of John the Baptist until now, the kingdom of the heavens is taken by violence, and the violent seize on it.

Dear Lord, we want to thank Thee for gathering us together here this morning. We thank Thee for Thy presence with us, and we do look to Thee to speak to us. Lord, we are all here waiting to hear from Thee. We pray that Thy Holy Spirit will open Thy Word to us and send Thy Word into our very heart. Do not allow us just to listen with our ears, Lord, but open our understanding that Thy Word may fall on good ground and bear fruit to Thyself a hundredfold. We ask in Thy precious name. Amen.

Once again I would like for you to join me in meditating on the Word of God. We must not just read it or hear it but ponder upon it before the Lord. We need to allow the Word of God really to be open to us and sink very deep into our hearts.

ONE GOSPEL—MANY FACETS

Before we meditate together, I would like to clarify one point. We are talking about the gospel of the kingdom of God, but we need to remember that the gospel of Jesus Christ is only one gospel. There are no other gospels. The apostle Paul made this very emphatic in Galatians: "If anyone should preach another gospel [of another kind,] he is to be cursed" because there is only one glad tiding and that glad tiding is our Lord Jesus Himself.

But our Lord Jesus is so full and so rich. Therefore, in the New Testament we find the gospel according to Matthew, the gospel according to Mark, the gospel according to Luke, and the gospel according to John. Now that does not mean we have four gospels. There is only one gospel. It is the gospel of Jesus Christ. But our Lord Jesus is so rich, you have to look at Him from different directions. So in the gospel of Matthew He is described as King, in Mark as Servant, in Luke as the perfect Man, and in John as perfect God.

When you look into the nature of the gospel of Jesus Christ, you find it has a number of different facets. The gospel of Matthew reveals the kingdom of God. The gospel of Mark shows us servanthood, how we should serve as servants of God. The gospel of Luke shows us grace, how the grace of God through our Lord Jesus has come to us. And the gospel of John shows us life, the eternal life of God through our Lord Jesus Christ. So the gospel of the kingdom is not another gospel of another kind; it is another of the same kind—the gospel of Jesus Christ.

Most believers are familiar with the gospel of Luke. We know Christ Jesus as our Savior. We receive the remission of our sins. It is grace that comes from our Lord Jesus. But unfortunately many of God's people do not know the gospel of the kingdom, that our Lord Jesus is more than Savior to us; He is our King. What does it mean for our Lord Jesus to be our King? How is it that we are in the kingdom of God? That is the reason we need to have more meditation on the gospel of the kingdom.

I want you to join with me in meditating as we concentrate on just one verse, Matthew 11:12: "But from the time of John the Baptist until now, the kingdom of the heavens is to be taken by violence, and the violent seize on it."

The kingdom of God is wherever God rules and reigns. Therefore His kingdom is from eternity to eternity. But strictly speaking, the kingdom of God is those who put themselves under the rule of God. In other words, God rules over all but some people are rebellious. Those who are obedient, who are submissive, who surrender and put themselves under the rule of God are truly in the kingdom of God.

Here you find the Scripture gives us a new term: *the gospel of the kingdom of the heavens.* In the whole Bible you can probably only find two places that are close to it. One is in Daniel 4:26: "The heavens do rule." That is the kingdom of the heavens. The only other place in the New Testament, aside from Matthew, is II Timothy 4:18. The apostle Paul said, "God will deliver me from every evil and he will preserve me for the heavenly kingdom." These are the only two places that are close to this term, *the kingdom of the heavens.* The *kingdom of the heavens* is a term used exclusively by Matthew, and you find it many times in his gospel. Some people say it is thirty-two times and others say it is thirty-three times, but it is a term used mostly in Matthew.

GOD OF THE HEAVENS AND EARTH

We would like to ask a question. Isn't God the God of the heavens and of the earth? If He is the God of the heavens and of the earth, then what is the need of specifically mentioning the kingdom of the heavens? You remember the story of the children of Israel in Babylonian captivity. During that period the Bible speaks of God as the God of the heavens, but He was not addressed as the God of the heavens and of the earth. Why? It is because during that period He had no representation on earth. The children of Israel, who were supposed to represent God on earth, were in captivity. They fell in their testimony. So far as the world was concerned it was as if God had retreated to heaven and was no longer on earth. He had no name on earth because Jerusalem was destroyed. The place where He put His name was destroyed. So during that period, He was always mentioned as the God of the heavens, and never as God of the earth, even though He is.

After the remnant came back, they rebuilt the temple. Yet very soon they degenerated and departed from God. Outwardly, they still maintained an appearance. They had rebuilt the temple, and the priesthood was serving. The law of God was in their midst, and they even had Pharisees and scribes who specialized in the letter of the law. But so far as their spiritual situation was concerned, they had departed from God.

So you remember, in the last book of the Old Testament, the book of Malachi, God had a controversy with His people. His people were blind and in darkness. They were insensitive to the love of God. They polluted His table and despised His name. They violated His covenant. They even robbed God of His due. That was the situation of the children of Israel—so-called God's people on earth—who were to represent God on earth. But what a failure! And the last

Word of God to His people was: "Return to Me that I may return to you."

REPENTANCE

After God had spoken this word, He was silent for four hundred years. There was no word from heaven to earth. But after four hundred years, suddenly God spoke again. John the Baptist began to proclaim the Word of God in the wilderness. The people flocked to the wilderness to hear him, and his message was: "Repent, for the kingdom of the heavens has drawn nigh." The children of Israel needed to repent, to turn around—not just a little bit of correction but an absolute turn around — because their direction was wrong. They were going in the wrong direction and they needed to turn back and return to God. Then God would return to them.

But God gave them a new reason for repentance. The reason for repentance is that the kingdom of the heavens has drawn nigh. In other words, it is as if God said, "You can go on your old way if you want to, but remember, the time has changed. The kingdom of the heavens is drawing nigh. If you do not repent and turn around, you will not have any part in the kingdom of the heavens." So you see that repentance is based upon the kingdom of the heavens.

Of course, we know what repentance is and that we need to repent of what we did wrong. But here you find the need to repent because something good, something excellent, something perfect is coming. This is a new reason for repentance. Do not think that you are good enough. You need to repent because when the kingdom of the heavens comes, your good is not good enough to enter in. You need to completely change your course, change your heart, circumcise your heart, return to God, and then there is hope for you. So here you find the term *the kingdom of the heavens*.

THE HEAVENS DO RULE

What is meant by the kingdom of the heavens? In our meditation, this is the first thing we need to consider. Is it different from the kingdom of God? Or is it the same? If it is the same, why use something different? We mentioned before that *kingdom* in the strictest sense, in the Scriptural sense, basically, means "kingship." In other words, it is the rule of the King, not in an external sense but more in an inward sense. That is to say, all those who are under His kingship, under His rule, begin to take up the character of the King. So the kingdom is the corporate expression of the King Himself. He expresses His nature and His character in a people, and that people are like Him. That is the kingdom. So the kingdom of God means those people who are under His rule. They take up God's character. They are like God. God is able to express Himself through this people, so they are His kingdom.

What is meant by the kingdom of the heavens? It means that the heavens rule over this people. This people are under heaven's rule, and heaven begins to be manifested in their lives. They live a heavenly life on earth. Then they are in the kingdom of the heavens. Now the kingdom of the heavens and the kingdom of God are parallel at times but not all times. The kingdom of God is from eternity to eternity, because even in the strictest sense from eternity to eternity there is no lack of people or angels who put themselves completely under the rule of God in spite of rebellions. So the kingdom of God is from eternity to eternity. But the kingdom of the heavens is one part in the kingdom of God, and in that one period the terms are interchangeable, according to the Word of God. Except for that one period of time in eternity, the kingdom of God is larger than the kingdom of the heavens.

To put it very simply, the kingdom of the heavens began with the first coming of our Lord Jesus. He who was in heaven has now come upon earth. He brought heaven down to set up His kingdom upon this earth. So the kingdom of the heavens began with the first coming of our Lord Jesus, and it ends with His second coming, when He shall come and set up His kingdom upon earth. The millennial kingdom is the kingdom of the heavens in manifestation. So to make it simple just keep in mind that the kingdom of the heavens is that section in the kingdom of God that begins with the first coming of Christ and ends with His second coming.

HEAVEN CAME DOWN TO EARTH

Why is it called the kingdom of the heavens? It is because He who was in heaven came down to earth. He brings heaven to earth. You remember our Lord Jesus said that He who was in heaven has come upon this earth and yet He is still in heaven (see John 3:13). He brings heaven with Him. He lives a heavenly life. He obeys the Father in the heavens. He *is* the King of the kingdom of the heavens.

But strangely, when John the Baptist began to preach, he said, "Repent for the kingdom of the heavens has drawn nigh." In other words, it is coming, it is near, but it had not arrived yet. At that time our Lord Jesus was on the earth, but He was not manifested yet. He was hidden in Nazareth for thirty years. John the Baptist began his ministry six months ahead of our Lord Jesus' ministry. So when he proclaimed the kingdom of the heavens, he could not say the kingdom of the heavens is here. He said, "The kingdom of the heavens has drawn nigh," because the King was still hidden. He was anonym (anonymous). He had not manifested Himself. But because the kingdom was near, there needed to be preparation for the King. That is repentance. The only preparation for the King of the heavens is repentance. We often think of repentance as something for unbelievers, but the children of Israel, who were supposed to be God's people, needed to repent.

And today, even we who believe in the Lord Jesus need to repent. It may not be for negative reasons, but if there are negative reasons we need to repent. But more, we need to repent for positive reasons—for the King, for the kingdom of the heavens, because our life on earth does not agree with the heavenly kingdom. We need to repent.

A KING WITHOUT DISCIPLES

"From the days of John the Baptist, until now." We know that John began his ministry probably around 27 AD. Six months later our Lord Jesus was baptized and began to minister. The Bible says that when He heard that John the Baptist was in prison (28 AD), our Lord Jesus began His public ministry in Galilee. When He began His public ministry, He said the same thing as John the Baptist: "Repent for the kingdom of the heavens has drawn nigh." Why? The King has come forward, so we might think He would say, "Repent, for the kingdom of the heavens is here." No. He said, "The kingdom of the heavens has drawn nigh." He preached the same message because the King was here, but where was His kingdom? Who were the people putting themselves under His kingship? Who were the people taking upon themselves the character of Christ? To put it another way, where were His disciples? A King without a people does not have a kingdom. So even though He was the King, yet His message was: "The kingdom of the heavens has drawn nigh."

JOHN'S IMPRISONMENT

We know that John the Baptist was in prison in 28 AD, and the story in Matthew 11 occurred in 29 AD, not quite two years later. It was during that time John the Baptist would soon be beheaded. So he sent his disciples to our Lord Jesus. His faith was so tested. He had not yet lost his faith in the Messiah, in Jesus, but he began to falter. So he sent his disciples to Jesus and asked,

"Are You really the One we are waiting for or should we wait for another one?"

John the Baptist had given such a wonderful testimony to our Lord Jesus, so sure and so clear: "Behold the Lamb of God who takes away the sin of the world. I saw the Spirit descend upon Him and abide in Him, and I was told He is the Son of God" (See John 1:29, 32).

John the Baptist said, "He must increase and I must decrease." That is such a clear testimony, and yet he was tested to the uttermost. He was in prison and the One whom he testified of did not seem to care. "Why did He do all these miracles to other people and not to me?" He was almost offended. When the Lord Jesus heard this, he said, "Tell John what I am doing. Yes, I opened the eyes of the blind; I made the cripple to walk; I preached the gospel to the poor; and I raised people from the dead. I am doing that, but I am not doing it to you. Will you be offended? I treat you special because I know you are able to bear it. You will not be offended by Me." And sure enough, John was faithful to the end.

DISCIPLESHIP

It was during that time that our Lord Jesus said, "From the days of John the Baptist until now..." *Now* has come. "The kingdom of the heavens is to be taken by violence, and the violent seize upon it." During that very particular time, there was a change. The kingdom of the heavens has not just drawn nigh, but the kingdom of the heavens is now here. Why? At that time the Lord already had His disciples. What does being His disciple mean? What does being discipled to Christ mean? To be discipled to Christ means you have put yourself completely under His rule. You allow Him to teach you. You allow Him to change you. You allow Him to transform you. You allow Him to let His character be impressed and implanted in you. That is discipleship.

In the old days the disciples were different from the students of today. Students of today go to school to the teacher. They listen to the lectures and try to absorb all he knows; and that is it. They do not learn from the teacher his life, his manner, or his character. It does not matter.

Everything is impersonal. But in the old days a disciple was different. If you wanted to learn a trade, you had to leave your home and live with your master. You became one of the master's family. You lived there. During the first year, he might not even tell you about the trade. You would do different things in the family—sweep the floor, help with the babies, or serve the master as a slave, as a servant. Gradually, he would allow you to touch the tools and would tell you some secrets. But through the years you would learn more than a trade; you would learn your master. You would begin talking like him, thinking like him, walking like him. You would begin to take up his manner. You would learn not only his skill but also his life. That is discipleship.

Here you find our Lord Jesus had called some to be His disciples. He called Peter, Andrew, John, James, Philip, Nathanael, and Matthew. They began to leave everything to stay with Him and learn of Him. So He already had His kingdom. He had a people under Him absolutely.

WHO IS OUR KING?

The *now* began at that time and it continues even to now. We are still in the *now*. The kingdom of the heavens is now here. It cannot be seen by naked eyes. It is still hidden in the world, but it is here. Wherever there are people who put themselves under the absolute rule of the King of the heavens, heaven begins to appear in their lives.

Thank God, when we believe in the Lord Jesus, it is more than just a personal forgiveness. Something much more was done when we were first saved. When we first believed in the Lord Jesus, we did not know much. We only knew Him as our Savior. We did not know Him as our King, and yet God had already done something to us.

In Colossians 1:13 it says, "He has delivered us from the power of darkness and has translated us into the kingdom of the Son of his love." What is the kingdom of the Son of God's love? It is the kingdom of the heavens, because the Son of God's love came from heaven. He brought heaven to earth, and He will set up His kingdom on earth. So positionally we are all in the kingdom of the heavens.

The kingdom of the heavens has taken us in, but have we taken the kingdom in? Positionally, we are all in the kingdom of the heavens, but conditionally, experientially, are we really living under the rule of heaven? Do we still live our old life? Do we still follow the way of the world? Have we really walked a heavenly way? We are a heavenly people on earth, but do we walk a heavenly life? Who is our king? Who is ruling our life? Whose character is being built up in us and manifested through us? These are questions we should meditate upon. We should ponder them, think over them. We should place ourselves in the light of heaven and allow that light to enlighten us.

Who Takes the Kingdom?

The kingdom of the heavens is now here, but who seizes upon it? Our Lord Jesus said, "The kingdom of the heavens is to be taken by violence and the violent seize on it." These are strong words. I have gone over many different versions to see if there are any softer, gentler, kinder, easier words, but unfortunately, I could not find any.

These versions may use different words. Some say, "violence" while others say, "force." Some say "violent" and others say "forceful." Some say "stormy." "The kingdom of the heavens is to be taken by storm, and the eager ones lay hold on it." All these words are strong words—military words, militant. Take the kingdom, seize it, storm it, just as you would take a city or a citadel. Storm it! Put all your force into it in order to seize it and capture it.

The kingdom of the heavens will not be taken by sitting in a sedan chair and being carried into it. That is the way God's people think, but it will not happen. It is to be taken by violence, and the violent seize on it. Why is it so? Is it easy to go to heaven? Yes, you do not need to do anything. You are carried to heaven. It is all by grace. Even if you try to do something, it may jeopardize you. It is better that you do nothing but trust in the Lord Jesus Christ.

THE KINGDOM OF THE HEAVENS IS PRECIOUS

The kingdom of the heavens is different. It has to be seized; it has to be taken. If you do not do that it will slip by. Why? I believe there are two reasons. One is positive. The kingdom of the heavens is so precious; it is a prize beyond measure. It is a treasure, and therefore it is not cheap. You have to pay a cost to take it. Our Lord Jesus is so precious. In order to win Him, in order to gain Him, there is something you have to do. The kingdom of the heavens is so precious that you have to pay a cost for it. There is no cheap gospel or cheap grace. Grace should embolden us to lay hold of eternal life. That is the attitude we should take.

We cannot afford to be complacent. We cannot afford to lay back and take it easy, as if it will just drop to us. No! You have to take it, seize it, storm into it, and pay a price for it because it is so precious. Do you see the preciousness of the kingdom of the heavens? Do you see the glory of being like Christ? Do you see the glory of suffering with Him that we may reign with Him? Isn't it something so glorious, so beautiful, and so attractive that you are willing to pay any cost to gain it? That is the kingdom of the heavens.

OVERCOMING OPPOSITION

Negatively, the kingdom of the heavens is very different from the kingdom of this world. Everything is different—different rule, different law, different manner, different criteria, different standard; everything is different. And because everything is different from earth, there is opposition, resistance, and persecution. There is much opposition you need to overcome—not only the temptations of the world, but most of all you need to overcome your self because our self is so selfish, worldly, and carnal. Our thinking, our emotion, our opinion—everything is contaminated by earth, sin, and flesh. All these are opposite to the kingdom of the heavens. And these oppositions have to be overcome. That is the reason our Lord Jesus said, "Unless you deny yourself, take up your cross and follow Me, you are not worthy to be My disciple."

The kingdom of the heavens is not for cowards. It is for those who have a lion heart. In the Bible you find again and again it says, "Be strong in the Lord and in the might of His strength." Be courageous, be a man. It is not for weaklings.

For these two reasons the kingdom of the heavens has to be taken by violence. But the violence here is a heavenly violence, not an earthly violence. We have seen enough violence on earth—violence to other people and kindness to yourself. But this heavenly violence is being violent to self and kind to others.

Are you doing violence to yourself? Why is our Christian life so weak? A little something can change our course. For a small reason we can leave God behind. Why? We do not do violence to ourselves.

THE LIFE OF OUR LORD JESUS

Look at our Lord Jesus. Look at the life of the heavenly Man on earth, the Man who brings heaven to earth. He is so different, altogether different from the world, not only from the worst but also from the best of the world. He is different. He thinks differently. He talks differently. He acts and reacts differently. He works differently. He sees things differently. And because He is different, He is misunderstood, rejected, persecuted, and crucified. The world is not worthy of such a Man. This is the King of the kingdom of the heavens.

THE LIFE OF PAUL

Look at Paul. After he was met by the risen Lord, he surrendered his life to the Lord. Did he have an easy life? No. How he suffered! He told us he put his body underneath, beat it black and blue, so that his body would not be master over him, that he would be the master of his body. Do we do that? For the sake of winning Christ, he forsook everything and counted all things as dross in order to win Christ. How he pressed on towards the goal to win the prize! That is violence; that is seizing the kingdom. Are we doing that?

PRESS ON TO GAIN THE KINGDOM

Our Christian life is too easy. We do not apply ourselves. We are not diligent. We are not paying any price. And do you think we can enter into the kingdom when it shall be publicly manifested at the second coming of our Lord Jesus? Do you think we are qualified to rule with Christ for a thousand years?

Truth is costly. It is not easy. If we press on we shall be in glory when He returns. If we do not, when His kingdom is publicly manifested on earth, we will be cast into outer darkness, as the Bible says. Even though we are saved, we are but barely saved.

So we need to be warned. The time is near, but we still have a chance. Surrender your life to the Lord. Let Him have absolute rule over you, and you will discover that there are so many lessons you have to learn. You will be humbled and humiliated beyond measure, but thank God, if we humble ourselves under the mighty hand of God, in due time He will exalt us. So let us be encouraged instead of discouraged. God bless.

Dear Lord, You always mean business with us. Therefore You sacrificed Your life for us. We pray that Thou wilt enable us to mean business with Thee, that we will be willing to put all on the altar for You. It is for Your pleasure, O Lord. We ask in Thy glorious name. Amen.

THE KINGDOM OF THE HEAVENS

Matthew 5:3—Blessed are the poor in spirit, for theirs is the kingdom of the heavens.

Matthew 13:11—And Jesus answering said to them [His disciples], Because to you it is given to know the mysteries of the kingdom of the heavens, but to them it is not given.

Matthew 24:42—Watch therefore, for ye know not in what hour your Lord comes.

Dear Lord, as we continue to worship Thee, we want to praise and thank Thee, knowing that Thou who hast come into this world and offered Thyself as the Lamb of God for the sin of the world, that Thou hast risen from the dead, ascended on high, and Thou art coming back again. We worship Thee because Thou art the King of kings and the Lord of lords. Even though the world does not know Thee, and yet Lord, by Thy grace we who are redeemed, we know that Thou art not only our Savior, Thou art our King. Teach us how to serve Thee, how to manifest Thy

Kingship in our lives, that we may glorify Thee. We commit this time into Thy hands and trust Thy Holy Spirit to guide us in our meditation. We ask in Thy precious name. Amen.

The kingdom of the heavens is a very special term in the Scripture. It is one section in the kingdom of God, for the kingdom of God is from eternity to eternity. And the kingdom of the heavens is that section in the kingdom of God that runs from the first coming of our Lord Jesus, the King of the heavens, to this earth, and ends with His second coming to set up His kingdom upon the earth.

The kingdom of the heavens has special relationship with us believers, His disciples, the church. So it is very, very important that we have a clear understanding of what the kingdom of the heavens is and how much it means to each one of us. It governs our daily life as Christians, and it determines our future destiny. So it has everything to do with us believers. I feel that we cannot move on to other things until we have a very clear understanding and appreciation of what the kingdom of the heavens is. So I would like to continue meditating together on the kingdom of the heavens, not in the sense that I preach and you listen. That is not the way. I want brothers and sisters to join with me together meditating on what the kingdom of the heavens is to us.

THE SCOPE OF THE KINGDOM OF THE HEAVENS

We know that the gospel according to Matthew is the gospel of the kingdom. In Matthew you have a full scope of what the kingdom of the heavens is. This is a special term used by Matthew, and in the book of Matthew there are three peaks concerning the kingdom of the heavens.

Matthew 5—7 is the revelation of the nature, the reality, and the eternal truth of the kingdom of the heavens—what the kingdom of the heavens really is. In Matthew 13 you have the mysteries of the kingdom of the heavens spoken by our Lord in parables. It tells us of the development, the history of the kingdom of the heavens as it is in this world. It is only understood by those who are the disciples of our Lord Jesus. It is not meant to be understood by the world. The world looks at the kingdom of the heavens as a mystery; they cannot understand it. But we, who are the Lord's, should understand how it is developed through history. Matthew 24—25, the so-called Olivet discourse, is a prophecy our Lord gave as to the coming of the kingdom of the heavens upon this earth, the public manifestation of that kingdom. So, in the gospel of Matthew you find the whole scope of the kingdom of the heavens.

THE NATURE OF THE KINGDOM OF THE HEAVENS

In Matthew 5—7, the so-called Sermon on the Mount, our Lord is not speaking to the multitudes. The Bible says the multitudes came to Him, but He spoke to His disciples. The multitudes overheard it, but it is the disciples to whom our Lord addressed this so-called Sermon on the Mount.

The Sermon on the Mount is not a new law. Moses gave the Law, and people say that our Lord Jesus gave a new law. Not at all, because no one can keep such words. Our Lord does not expect anyone to be able to keep the words that

He spoke in Matthew 5—7. The more you try to keep these words, the more you realize it is humanly impossible. So what is the Sermon on the Mount? The Lord is telling us what the kingdom of the heavens really is, what His kingship really is, and how people who are discipled to Him take upon themselves the character of the King of the heavens. That is what it is. In other words, it is grace; it is not law. No one can do it, but grace is well able to transform us into the likeness of our King and, in doing that reveal the kingdom of the heavens. That is Matthew 5—7.

Matthew 5 shows us the product of His grace, what His grace has done in His people. Matthew 6 tells us the process—how it works, how it comes about that people like we are can be transformed and become like what He is. And Matthew 7 tells us how to possess it. In other words, what is our response, our responsibility to the grace of God? We are not able to deal in details, so out of these three chapters we will take only one verse to meditate on together.

I looked up the word *meditate*. The word *meditate* in Greek surprised me. I always thought of *meditate* as a matter of the mind. We use our mind to meditate. But it surprised me because the word *meditate* in Greek, first of all, means "to set your heart on it, to practice it." Meditation is more than a matter of the mind; it is a matter of the heart. That is the reason why in Psalm 19 it is said, "May the words of my mouth and the meditation of my heart be acceptable to thee." Meditation is more than using your mind; it is using your heart. You set your heart upon it, and then ponder over it, not with your natural mind but with your renewed mind. That is meditation.

Our Lord Jesus said, "Blessed are the poor in spirit, for theirs is the kingdom of the heavens." Who does the kingdom of the heavens belong to? What is the kingdom of the heavens, the kingdom of the heavenly King? Who are they? It says, "Blessed are the poor in spirit, for theirs is the kingdom of the heavens."

The so-called Beatitudes actually are a picture of what the King of the heavens is. These Beatitudes tell us the character of the King and that His character is to characterize those who are in His kingdom.

THE POOR IN SPIRIT

"Blessed are the poor in spirit." When you hear of the kingdom of the heavens, it may not impress you as glad tidings at all. It seems to be hard, difficult, demanding a lot, and full of conditions. You have to struggle for it; the violent take it. It does not sound like a gospel, a glad tiding; but it is a glad tiding. "Blessed are the poor in spirit, for theirs is the kingdom of the heavens." The word *blessed* means "happy." "Happy are the poor in spirit, for theirs is the kingdom of the heavens."

When you hear the message, you may say, "Well, there is not much happiness in it. It takes away your happiness. It is so difficult." But this is *true* happiness. You do not know true joy, true happiness until you are poor in spirit. And we are to be put in that blessed position. Naturally, we are all proud people. Do not think that you are humble. When people say, "Look how humble I am," you know that is the expression of extra-ordinary pride.

THE SIN OF PRIDE

What is sin? How does sin come about? That archangel Lucifer began to think of himself. He was created by God in such beauty, so talented. He was put in the highest place as a cherub on the throne of God. He was supposed to lead the angels, the angelic host, to worship and sing praises unto God. He was given great power and authority, but instead of being conscious only of God his Creator, he began to look upon himself. How beautiful! How talented! How powerful! What position! What authority! He began to be self-conscious. The more he was conscious of himself, the prouder and the more ambitious he became. He wanted to be equal with God. That is how sin came into the world.

And the same thing happened to mankind. God created Adam and Eve in His image, according to His likeness for the glory of God, to obey God, to honor God, and to keep His commandments. Yet man began to think of himself: "I want to be God. I am over all the creatures, but that is not enough. I want to be God."

Pride, self-consciousness, self-importance, self-glory—that is the root of all sins. This is the spirit of the world, of the kingdom of this world. They respect and even worship those who are proud and arrogant, who have charisma, who are able to project themselves above other people, who are ambitious, seeking for themselves. These are the people the world respects. This is the spirit of the kingdom of this world. This is how we are. We are born with this pride. We think of ourselves more than anything else.

If you think you are humble, wait until someone says something that you think you do not deserve. Why do you think you do not deserve such criticism? It is because you think you are much better than that. Isn't that pride? Why is it we are hurt when people criticize us? That is pride. It is in our very constitution; we cannot help it. But the kingdom of the heavens is entirely different. "Blessed are the poor in spirit." It is not haughty spirit, not like the Laodiceans who said, "We are rich, lacking nothing. We have everything." Poor in spirit is such character, such a trait that is not earthly. You cannot find it on earth. It comes from heaven. When the King of the heavens visited this earth, He brought that character to this world.

THE CHARACTER OF THE KING

You remember Philippians 2:5-8: "He being equal with God, and that is not something to be grasped at." In other words, that is His right, and yet He emptied Himself of all the glory and honor and worship that are His by right. He could not empty His deity because that is what He is. He is God forever, but He put aside everything connected with deity and took up the form of a bondslave. That is inward feeling, poor in spirit.

"And being in the fashion of a man He was obedient to the Father, even unto death, and that the death of the cross." "Poor in spirit." You can only find it in Christ Jesus, the King of the heavens. You would think of the King as riding on a horse, commanding, demanding, being served, but the Lord said that in the kingdom of the heavens it is different. He came to serve, not to be served, and to give His life as a ransom for many. "Poor in spirit." That is where you can find it.

Why is it that "poor in spirit" is placed first in the Beatitudes? Of course, when you think of God, probably you would put love first because God is love. But in the Beatitudes "poor in spirit" is the first blessing because it concerns us. So far as we are concerned, this is where it must begin. All the other qualities of Christ that are to be impressed and become ours come after this one quality of being "poor in spirit." Only when you are poor in spirit will all the rest of the blessings follow. And that is the reason it is put as the first blessing.

THE WORK OF THE HOLY SPIRIT

How can we do it, we who are naturally proud, even though we have almost nothing? This is beyond us. We cannot do it. It is the work of God, the work of the Holy Spirit. When the Holy Spirit works the character of our King into our lives, He works two ways. Positively, He will reveal the glory and the beauty of the King to us. You do not know how poor you are until you really see the wealthy. You do not know how ugly you are until you meet the real beauty. We often compare ourselves with other people whom we consider as inferior to us. Why? Why not compare with superior people? It is because of pride. A revelation of the beauty of the Lord reduces our beauty to ashes.

A Vision of Christ

You remember Daniel. Daniel is like a perfect person. Who can compare with Daniel? He was Prime Minister of the greatest empire in the world at that time. He managed so many things, but his enemy could not find any fault by which to accuse him. And yet in Daniel 10, when he saw the glory of the Lord, he said, "My beauty turned into corruption."

The reason we are not poor in spirit, the reason why we are proud and haughty in spirit is because we have not seen the Lord. We always compare ourselves with other brothers and sisters. But once the Spirit of God reveals Christ to you, then your beauty turns into corruption. You will no longer boast of your strength or of your beauty. You will fall down before Him as if dead. Our problem is that we see ourselves, we see others, but we do not see Christ. That is our problem. Who is willing to let go of himself? Who is willing to acknowledge that he is nobody unless he sees the One who is perfect?

The Cross

We need to have a revelation, a vision of our Lord Jesus. That is what we need because only that can humble us. But then when the Holy Spirit gets to work, it is more than just revealing to us the beauty of our Lord; He also works in us the work of emptying. He begins to empty us of all that we boast of, all that we consider as our beauty and our strength. He begins to apply the cross into our lives. It is a painful process, but it is a necessary one because it makes room to be filled with Christ. So the working of the cross in our lives is necessary to make room for Christ. We are so full of ourselves. We are so full of our opinions. We are so full of self-seeking. All these have to go. We have to be reduced in order to increase, but what is increased is no longer ourselves; it is Christ. So we say that it is the work of the Holy Spirit, but it needs our cooperation. We need to be willing. We need to allow the Holy Spirit to work in our lives, and if we are willing, He will do it.

Deny Self

Some people may say, "If I am reduced I will become nobody. Isn't that very pessimistic and negative? Where is my personality?" True, if you try to reduce yourself and make yourself *like* "poor in spirit" that is what will happen. You will despise yourself—no self-esteem, no self-respect anymore: "I am nobody; I am nothing; I am finished."

If you do it yourself, that is what will happen. But if it is the work of the Holy Spirit, there is a difference. Why? On the one hand it is true, He brings you to know yourself in a real way, and when you know yourself in the real way, you *do* despise it.

Do you ever despise yourself? If you have never despised yourself, you do not know yourself. Indeed, under the light of heaven, you despise yourself. You do want to know Him, and that is what *deny* self means. Deny yourself. Why do you deny yourself? It is because you do not want to know him; it is a shame. But thank God, it is not negative at all because Christ's life and His character begins to build up in you for the glory of God—not for you. And when you are brought into that state you are really happy. Do you know why you are not happy? You have too much of yourself. When you are free from yourself and Christ fills your heart, you are in a blessed position, in a happy mood. The kingdom of the heavens is yours. So let us meditate more on it until the Lord's work is done in our lives. That is the Sermon on the Mount.

THE MYSTERIES OF THE KINGDOM OF THE HEAVENS

Then in Matthew 13 our Lord Jesus moves on. After the Pharisees and the scribes blasphemed the Holy Spirit in Matthew 12, when our Lord addressed the multitudes, He no longer spoke openly but He used parables. *Parable* means "playing alongside." It is a familiar scene to illustrate something with a deeper and spiritual meaning. That is a parable. So our Lord Jesus began to speak in parables. And when He did that, His disciples came to Him and said, "Why do You speak in parables and not in plain words?" Our Lord said, "Because the mysteries of the kingdom of the heavens are for you to understand, not for the world."

So far as the world is concerned, the kingdom of the heavens is a mystery. It is something hidden. It is a secret unknown unless it is explained. But to us, to the disciples of our Lord Jesus, He explains; He opens our understanding because we are supposed to know such mysteries. Now, do you know these parables?

These parables are very important because they tell us of the historical development of the kingdom of the heavens upon this earth. This is hidden from the world and yet our Lord opens it up to us who are His so that we can understand how it develops. Since the coming of our Lord Jesus, the kingdom of the heavens has been brought down from heaven to earth, and He is gradually building up that kingdom. And the process is shown us in Matthew 13.

The Parable of the Sower

These seven parables (or eight) are continuous. They have a continuous character in them. The first parable is the parable of the sower. The sower is none other than our Lord Jesus Himself. He came into this world to sow the word of the kingdom, which is the seed. The fields are the hearts of men. When the word of the kingdom of the heavens is sown into the hearts, unfortunately only one of the four is a prepared ground to receive the word. With patience it began to bear fruit. That is the beginning of the history of the kingdom of the heavens on earth.

The Wheat and the Darnel

The second parable is the wheat and the darnel. In this parable you find a progression. The wheat, the seed that the sower has sown, has become the sons of the kingdom of the heavens. In other words, the word of the kingdom of the heavens has been received and it began to change these people to become sons of the kingdom of the heavens. And they are sown in this world, which is the field. The sons of the kingdom of the heavens are everywhere. And the enemy came and sowed in the same field (the world) darnel (sons of the wicked one), and they grew together. This was done without the knowledge of the servants, but of course, the master knew it. In other words, our Lord knew all along, but His people did not know it. But when they grew up, the servants began to realize it, and they came to the Lord and said, "Who did it? What should we do with it? Should we pull them all out?" "No, leave them alone because if you pull out the darnel you will pull out the wheat too, because their roots began to intertwine. Wait until the harvest time."

What is this? This is the outward appearance of the kingdom of the heavens on this earth today. It is a picture of Christianity. It is a picture of Christendom. Whenever the gospel is preached, wherever the influence of the gospel goes, whether it is a hospital, a school, or something else, you find Christianity began to spread. And in Christianity you have mixture. People profess to be Christians, but they are false brothers. You cannot pull them out. If you do, you will pull everything out. You have to wait until harvest time, which is the end of the world. And it is not the work of man; it is the work of the angels. Our Lord will send His angels to sort them out, burn the darnel, and bring the wheat into the garner. That is the second parable. Do you see the development here?

The Outward Appearance of the Kingdom

Then you have the third and fourth, and fifth and sixth parables. These two pairs are contrasts. The third and fourth tell us the abnormal growth of the outward appearance of the kingdom of the heavens because a mustard seed is the smallest seed, living. Our Lord said that if you have faith like a mustard seed, you can remove the mountain because it is living. Mustard is a vegetable, and yet this mustard seed has grown to be a huge tree of abnormal growth. And because of this, all the birds came and roosted in it. In the first parable, you remember the birds represent the devil; so in this parable it is the same. In other words, you find Christianity has outgrown its nature. It became an abnormal growth, and has become a big institution in this world. All kinds of evil find a nest. That is the outward.

The inward is the fourth parable. The woman put the leaven into three meals of wheat. Three meals of wheat were supposed to be a meal offering to God, but it should not be leavened. But here a leaven is put in, and it blows up with corrupt teaching and heresies. All kinds of teachings corrupted the gospel of Jesus Christ. That is what the outward appearance of the so-called kingdom of the heavens is in this world.

The Hidden Ones of the Kingdom

But thank God, there are the fifth and sixth parables, the treasure and the pearl. These represent that even in this confusion the real thing is still there—the hidden ones. They are hidden to the world but known to Christ. And for that He gave all to possess them. Treasure speaks of the truth; pearl speaks of the experience that is of God. And that is the reality within. In spite of the abnormal growth, the corruption within, God still has His hidden ones.

The Dragnet

Finally, there is the dragnet, which is the end of the world. Everything will be separated. That is the history of the kingdom of the heavens upon this earth, and our Lord wants us to know it. But to the world it is still a mystery. They do not know it.

THE KINGDOM IS ESTABLISHED ON EARTH

Finally, in Matthew 24—25 our Lord prophesied how the kingdom of the heavens will eventually be established upon this earth, when the kingdom of this world shall become the kingdom of the Lord and of His Christ. Oh, brothers and sisters, do not think that our Lord is not working. Do not think that the kingdom of the heavens will never be publicly established upon this earth. Though He is in heaven at the right hand of the Father, He is not sleeping; He is working. The Bible tells us He is working. He is opening the seals. He is working to bring His kingdom in, to make the kingdom of this world the kingdom of God and of His Christ. He is working. We can be assured of that. There will be lots of tribulations, lots of conflicts, because the enemy does not want to give up, but he has no chance. His end is coming.

All the signs given show us it is near, nearer than you think. Our Lord can come at any moment. All the prophecies before the coming of the Lord have all been fulfilled. There are prophecies still to be fulfilled, but these prophecies will be fulfilled *at* the coming of the Lord, *during* the coming of the Lord, and *after* the coming of the Lord. But so far as *before* the coming of the Lord, all prophecies have been fulfilled. It can happen any moment, but we do not know the time.

PREPARE FOR THE KINGDOM

So what is the word of the Lord to us? Watch therefore; do not go to sleep. Do not be complacent. Do not allow the world to take away your heart. Seek ye first the kingdom of God and His righteousness. Do violence to yourself that you may seize on it. Be poor in spirit, for theirs is the kingdom of the heavens. Be prepared for it. And if you are ready at any time, when He suddenly comes, you will be with Him.

Do you see how important is the kingdom of the heavens? If we do not live in the kingdom of the heavens today, when the kingdom of the heavens is openly, publicly, universally established upon this earth, where will you be? You will be cast into outer darkness; that is to say, you will have no part in the kingdom of the heavens. You cannot reign with Christ for a thousand years. You cannot enter into the joy of the Lord. You will be gnashing your teeth with regret. *For the love of a moment, you sacrifice the glory of a thousand years.* That does not mean you are not saved; you are saved. In eternity you will be in the heavenly Jerusalem, but you will have no part in the kingdom of the heavens during that thousand years.

So, brothers and sisters, let's meditate on it. Set your heart upon it. Practice it. Ponder over it. Do not allow this just to drift away. It has everything to do with you today and tomorrow. So may the Lord have mercy upon us, knowing that His grace is sufficient.

Shall we pray:

Dear Lord, we want to thank Thee because Thy heart is for our happiness. Thou dost desire to bless. Oh, do remove from us everything that stands in the way of Thy blessing. Bring us into the position that Thou can really bless us with Thy blessing, and we want to bless Thee. In Thy precious name. Amen.

THE KINGDOM AND THE CHURCH

Matthew 16:18-19—And I also, [that is our Lord] I say unto thee that thou art Peter, [a rock, a stone, a little stone] and on this rock [this massive rock] I will build my church, and hades' gates shall not prevail against it. And I will give to thee the keys of the kingdom of the heavens; and whatsoever thou mayest bind upon the earth shall be bound in the heavens; and whatsoever thou mayest loose on the earth shall be loosed in the heavens.

Dear Lord, as we continue in Thy presence, we look to Thee to speak to us through Thy Word and by Thy Spirit. How we praise and thank Thee that Thou art One who is still speaking. Oh Lord, open our inner ears, open our hearts that we may understand what Thou art saying to us, and we may respond to Thee. Lord, as we come to the closing of this age, do prepare us for Thyself. We commit this time into Thy loving hands and look to Thee for Thy Word, Thy living Word. We ask in the precious name of our Lord Jesus. Amen.

We have been meditating together on some of the words of our Lord Jesus, especially on this matter of the kingdom of the heavens. We would like to continue in our meditation, and again I expect you brothers and sisters to join with me in our meditation. In other words, it is not that I am speaking and you are listening, but I want you all to be very active in your spirit and join with me in meditating together on the Word of our Lord Jesus.

We would like to meditate on the relationship between the church and the kingdom. In these two verses our Lord Jesus seemed to put these two subjects together. He said to Peter, "You are Peter [a stone]. On this rock I will build My church, and the gates of hades shall not prevail against it." Immediately, our Lord continues by saying, "I will give to you the keys of the kingdom of the heavens. Whatsoever you shall bind on earth shall be bound in heaven, and whatsoever you shall loose on earth shall be loosed in heaven."

We have before us two things—"My church" and "the kingdom of the heavens." Of course, when our Lord Jesus talks about the church, He does not mean what people ordinarily think about the church. Sometimes people think of the church as a place, as a building, built with material things. Other times people think of the church as an organization, an institution—a religious club, if we may say it. But when our Lord Jesus mentions this word *church*, He means exactly what it is, the called-out ones gathered together. "Where two or three are gathered together unto My name," our Lord said, "there am I in their midst." That is what the church really is. The church is His body, the body of Christ, and He is the Head of that body.

Likewise, when our Lord talks about the kingdom of the heavens, within the context we may understand, He does not refer to the outward appearance of the kingdom of the heavens to the world. We find that in Matthew 13 in the parables. But what He means is exactly what the kingdom of the heavens really is, and that is the Kingship of Christ. Our Lord Jesus, who is not only our Savior but also our King, shares His own character in a people who obey

Him, who belong to Him, and who become His kingdom.

So because these subjects are so wide, we have to limit them to the church in spiritual reality and the kingdom of the heavens in spiritual reality. When you look at them in that aspect you will find that the church and the kingdom of the heavens are one. They are the two sides of one coin.

THE KINGDOM BUILDS THE CHURCH

When you talk about the church, the emphasis is on life because Christ is living and His church is a living church. When you talk about the kingdom, the emphasis is on character because the character of the King characterizes His kingdom. All those who are the sons of the kingdom have the same character as the King. When you talk about the church, the important thing is "build." The Lord said, "I will build My church." In other words, the church needs to be built. It is not only to be born, but it is to be built. And when you talk about the kingdom of the heavens, the emphasis is on testimony. The kingdom of the heavens is a witness to the world in this age, and one day it will bring in that kingdom upon this earth.

After we have defined the scope that we would like to meditate on, then we can go on and meditate on the relationship between the church and the kingdom.

The Keys to Build

The Lord Jesus said, "I will build My church." But how is He going to build His church? It is followed immediately by what our Lord said, "I will give you the keys of the kingdom of the heavens." So immediately you begin to join these two words together. The church is built by using the keys of the kingdom of the heavens. We want to interpret the keys as the ways of building the kingdom and the ways of building the church

Usually when we talk about the keys of the kingdom of the heavens that our Lord gave to Peter, we say it refers to the fact that Peter was the first one who used the keys. And when he used the keys he was proclaiming the gospel. Once, he used the keys on the day of Pentecost to the Jews and the second time he used the keys to open the door to the Gentiles that they might be brought in. So we say "the keys" of the kingdom of the heavens is the preaching of the gospel.

When you think of the gospel, probably in your mind it means the gospel of grace. We are sinners with no hope, condemned eternally. But Christ Jesus came and shed His blood. He gave us His body. He became the Lamb of God to take away the sin of the world, and by believing in Him our sins are forgiven. We are given a new life; we are guaranteed heaven. Now that is the gospel we usually think about.

But when you look into what Peter preached on the day of Pentecost, as well as what he preached in the house of Cornelius, you find it is a little bit different. In other words, it is more; it is fuller. It is a full gospel because the gospel he preached is not only on the side of grace but also on the side of the kingdom. Why? You remember in Acts 2 when he concluded his message he said, "God has made Jesus, whom you have crucified, Lord and Christ." Now that is a kingdom message. He has become the King of kings and the Lord of lords. He is far above all, and because this is what He is, therefore we need to believe, and not only believe but obey. The gospel is to be obeyed, not just to be believed. In Romans 1:5 it says, "...the obedience to the gospel." Why? He is King; therefore, we need not only to believe in Him but also to obey Him. That is the message on the day of Pentecost.

In Acts 10 he began to give his message to the Gentiles. He did not finish it because the Holy Spirit came in and interrupted, but he had said, "This Jesus, God has made Him Judge over all people." That is more than the gospel of grace; that is the gospel of the kingdom. He is the Judge of all nations.

So when Peter used the keys of the kingdom of the heavens, when he preached the gospel to the people, there you find it brings in the church. The keys of the kingdom of the heavens open the door to the church because we believe in the Lord, we obey Him, and we receive new life. We are born into the family of God. But the same keys of the kingdom of the heavens are used for the building of the church. Let me explain.

Discipleship

Matthew 28:18-20: "And Jesus coming up spoke to them, saying, All power has been given me in heaven and upon earth. Go therefore and make disciples of all the nations, baptising them to the name of the Father, and of the Son, and of the Holy Spirit; teaching them to observe all things whatsoever I have enjoined you. And behold, I am with you all the days, until the completion of the age."

This is what we call the great commission. The great commission is based upon what the Lord said in verse 18: "All power has been given me in heaven and upon earth." Whenever you think of power or authority, you tie it with the kingdom. When our Lord Jesus ascended up on high, God has made Him King over all things. All power, all authority, both in heaven and upon earth, have been given to Him. That is the basis of the great commission. Otherwise we have no authority. We have no power to fulfill that commission. So first of all, we need to remember that the great commission is based upon the kingship of our Lord Jesus. It has to do with the kingdom.

Then He said, "Go." Throughout church history God's people began to hear this word, "Go." Go to all the world; go to every nation and preach the gospel. Bring people to salvation. Evangelize the nations. Unfortunately, this is only a part of the commission, not the full commission. If you read carefully, you find the Lord said, "Go." Go do what? Evangelize the world? No. "Go, make disciples of all nations." In other words, the great commission is a full commission; it is a full gospel that we have to go and preach. It is the gospel of the kingdom of the heavens because discipleship has something to do with the kingdom of the heavens. Go make disciples of all nations. It is not enough just to get people saved, as if heaven needs to be filled.

Why are we saved? For what purpose? Just for our own good? No. We are saved that God's purpose may be fulfilled in our lives. In order to do that we have to be discipled to Christ Jesus. It is not just believing in Him, but it is putting ourselves under His authority and allowing Him to transform us, change us, and conform us to His own image. That is discipleship. Discipleship always has to do with the kingdom, and it is through discipleship the church is built. The Lord said, "Go. Make disciples of all nations. Not only bring people to Me, but bring people to Me in such a manner that they really become My disciples, that I am able to disciple them, I am able to train them, I am able to complete them, and perfect them."

Baptism

In this matter of discipleship, the first thing mentioned in this commission is that our Lord said, "Baptizing them to the name of the Father, and of the Son, and of the Holy Spirit." Isn't that strange? The Lord said, "Make disciples of all nations." How are you going to make disciples? Teach them—is that the way to make disciples? No, the Lord said, "Baptizing them to the Father and the Son and the Holy Spirit." Why is it so? Why is baptism so important? You often hear people say, "Isn't it in the Word of God, 'Believe and you are saved'? So why should we be baptized?"

The reason is that it is the door to discipleship. He cannot disciple us until we are baptized to the name of the Father, the Son, and the Holy Spirit. What does it mean? What is baptism? In baptism we go into the water, we are immersed under the water, and we come up out of the water. What do all these symbolize? They symbolize death, burial, and resurrection. In baptism we proclaim that there is no good in this old man, this I, this self, this natural man. He needs to go to death, but you do not need to do it yourself because Christ has already died. And He died not only for you, but when He died, the Bible tells us that we died in Him.

Christ is the last Adam, the second Man. In Him all the Adamic race comes to an end because when the last Adam died, the Adamic race is terminated. The death of our Lord Jesus is all-inclusive. It is more than just our Lord as one person dying on the cross. When He died on the cross, He not only bore all the sins of the world, but He also brought all the sinners with Him to that cross. So in the sight of God, when Christ died, we all died. We died in Him. That is an eternal truth. That is something that God has done in His beloved Son. It is already finished, already done. And in baptism you confess that this old man of mine is already dead. There is no good in him. Anything, everything in this old man is not fit to be built into the body of Christ. It is a foreign article. It cannot be assimilated. It will be rejected no matter what you do. It should be completely set aside.

Brothers and sisters, do you realize that? You need to take the position by faith that God has already gotten rid of your old man—you, as you know, as everybody knows, you, this "I" died two thousand years ago in the cross of our Lord Jesus. You confess it, you believe it, you take that position, and you act it out by going under the water. Buried, out of sight. You do not want to see him anymore. He is gone forever.

But thank God, there is a coming out of the water, because Christ was buried for three days and three nights and then He was raised from the dead. And when He rose, you by faith are risen with Him in newness of life, not in oldness of law. In other words, by taking baptism that is saying good-bye to yourself, farewell. It is eternal separation. You come out of the water a new man in Christ Jesus. And it is this new life, this new man in Christ Jesus that can be trained, transformed, conformed to the image of Christ, and built into the body of Christ. That is what baptism means. That is why the Lord said, "Baptizing them to the name of the Father, the Son, and the Holy Spirit." Now you are no longer under your own name; you are under the name of the Father, the Son, and the Holy Spirit. You have changed your name. You know, it is just like when a woman marries a man, her name is changed. So in baptism we change our name from being of Adam to being now of Christ. And only standing on that ground are we able to be discipled.

Let me use an illustration. In the old days before there were schools, as we know today, how did a person learn a profession, a trade? You learned by being an apprentice. To be an apprentice is not an easy thing. Why? First of all, you have to leave your own home. You cannot stay at home and go to school. You have to be completely severed from your home and you are not allowed to come back without the permission of your master. You are not free anymore. You have to join yourself to your master's house. You become a member of your master's household. You stay with him maybe three years before you finish learning that trade. During the first year you stay in the master's home, he might not teach you anything about the trade. He might not even allow you to touch the tools. So what do you do there? You do all the mundane things—maybe sweep the floor, maybe serve the master at the table, maybe even help to carry the children. You do all these things that have nothing to do with your trade but are very important. Why? To learn the trade in the old days was more than learning a skill; it was to learn how to be a man. You watched your master—the way he talked, the way he did business, his relationships, actions, reactions, and attitudes—all these things. Gradually, he would allow you to touch the tools a little bit. He would teach you a little bit and you practiced it until you learned it. After you finished your apprenticeship, when you came out, you were a replica of your master. Not only had you learned his skills, you had learned him. You would talk like him. You would act like him and walk like him. Your voice would also have his tone. That is discipleship. In the Bible when you talk about discipleship, that is the idea.

So unless you are completely separated from the past, you are not able to enter into the new. That is the reason why baptism is the opening to discipleship. Brothers and sisters, we need to review our baptism. Why is it that it seems so hard for the Lord to change us? Why is it that our old habits, our old ways cling to us so strenuously? Why is it that they are so hard to shake off? It is because we have not taken the ground of discipleship. If you have taken this ground of discipleship, that is to say, you completely deny yourself and open yourself to your Master, to your King, to your Christ, allowing Him to do anything and everything He wants to, and has every right to do, how quickly you will be changed and transformed.

The Whole Counsel of God

Then, "Teach them to observe all things whatsoever I have enjoined you." Teach them all the counsel of God, the whole counsel of God. Just like Paul said, "I have not withheld anything from you. I have taught you the whole counsel of God." But what is the sense of teaching if it is not for the sake of observing? So he said, "Teaching them to observe. . . " It is not only teaching them to have a big mind. Knowledge, mental knowledge puffs up. But it is teaching them to observe, to do. God's teaching is to do, not just to think about. And when you observe all the things that Christ has taught, you will see a change begin in your life.

And the Lord said, "I am with you to the end of the age." You will experience the abiding presence of the Lord with you. That is the great commission.

The Headship of Christ

When you meditate, you meditate one word from the Word of God, and the Spirit of God will lead you to another word. That is the way to meditate. So, naturally we will be led to Colossians 2:19. But in Colossians 2:19 it is negative because it begins with *not*. It should not be, so we will read it in a positive way. "Holding fast the head, from whom all the body, ministered to and united together by the joints and bands, increases with the increase of God."

That is the building of the church, the building of the body. What is to be increased? It is not that you and I be increased; it is increased with the increase of God. In other words, in the body of Christ, you begin to see God is increased; Christ is increased in this people. It is not some people getting increased, but God is increased; Christ is increased.

How can it be done? The secret is holding fast the Head. Now we know that the Head here is singular in number. The Head is Christ. How can Christ be Head, the only Head, if all of us still have our own heads? That is impossible. So first of all, we have to be beheaded, not literally, but spiritually. We have to lay down our headship, that is to say, lay down our own mastership. We are our own master. We have our ways. We have our thoughts. We have our will. We have our opinions. We have our habits. All of these have to be laid down. We refuse to be head. We refuse to take the initiative. We submit ourselves under the headship of Christ and let Him be Head. So you see, this is the same as discipleship. It is the key of the kingdom of the heavens. That is the way to open the door to the building of the body of Christ.

What happens when we all honor the authority of the Head? All the body ministers to and is united together by the joints and bands. Some brothers and sisters are like joints. Joints are joints of supply. In other words, we are able to minister what the Lord has given us to the church, to the body of Christ. And some people are like bands, bands to unite. There are people who may not be able, in a sense, to minister much but they are able to bring people together in love. They are bands. Again you find all the joints and the bands will minister to and join together, and the result is that the body will increase with the increase of God. That is the secret of the building of the church, using the keys of the kingdom. Do you see the relationship between the kingdom and the church? The kingdom builds the church. Without accepting the kingdom, the kingship of Christ, the church cannot be built.

THE CHURCH BRINGS IN THE KINGDOM

Pray in the Kingdom

But then we have to go to the other side. What has the church to do with the kingdom? The kingdom builds the church, but the church brings in the kingdom. In Matthew 6:10, in the Lord's prayer, our Lord Jesus teaches the church to pray. Pray for what? "Thy kingdom come." It is the responsibility of the church to pray in the kingdom of the heavens upon this earth. That is how important prayer is. I believe we have been praying, but have we ever prayed, "Thy kingdom come"? Oh, how we pray, "Lord, let *my* will be done and *my* kingdom come." But the Lord said, "Pray, let *Thy* kingdom come."

The church is to pray in the kingdom of the heavens, but it is more than just praying. In Matthew 24:14 it says, "And these glad tidings of the kingdom shall be preached in the whole habitable earth, for a witness to all the nations, and then shall come the end."

It is the responsibility of the church to pray that the kingdom come. When you look at the kingdoms of this world—so confused, so violent, so terrifying, so lawless—do you feel urged to pray, "Lord, Thy kingdom come because Thy kingdom is different. When Thy kingdom shall come, all the swords shall be turned into plows. Even the animals will not eat each other. There will be peace, righteousness, and glory over this earth." Oh, how we need to pray, "Thy kingdom come." God will not do anything until His church begins to pray.

Preach the Kingdom

But we are not only to pray; we are to preach. The message of the kingdom of the heavens must be preached to all the nations as a witness; then the end will come. You know, in church history you find some people feel that the responsibility of the church, so far as the world is concerned, is to change the world. The church is to change the world and make it better, make it Christian, which is what post-millennialism really means. But is this the way to bring in the kingdom? We will preach the message of the kingdom of the heavens as a witness. In other words, we are not to change the world. God is not going to do that. God is going to judge the world. But we are to overcome the world, to overcome not by political or military or whatever; we are to overcome the world of all its evils.

The church in the eyes of God is an overcoming church. The church is supposed to overcome—overcome temptations, overcome evil, overcome all these unrighteous, unlawful things, and be a witness of the kingdom of the heavens in this corrupt world. That is our testimony. Our testimony is to show the world, in spite of what the world is today, that there is a better world, the kingdom of the heavens, and we are living in it. We are under the rule of heaven, overcoming evil as a testimony to the world. And that is why you find in the Word of God, when the bride of the Lamb has made herself ready, that is to say, when the church is built, when it begins to take up the full measure of the stature of Christ, as found in Ephesians 5, then the Bridegroom will come.

Overcomers

The building of the church is to bring in the kingdom, but unfortunately when you look at the church today, it is more like Laodicea. So what is God going to do? Will the church never be matured, never be grown up, and therefore the kingdom never come upon this earth? No. God's way is higher than man's way. You will find in the Word of God the principle of overcomers. "He that has an ear, let him hear what the Spirit says to the churches. He who overcomes . . ." Among God's people He is calling for overcomers. Who are those overcomers? The overcomers are none other than the normal Christians. We are so abnormal, so subnormal today, that God is calling us back to normalcy. What is a normal Christian? A normal Christian is a disciple of Christ. A normal Christian is one who puts himself under the headship of Christ. A normal Christian is one who allows the Lord to work His character in his or her life in spite of what is around him. What other people may do, you cannot. And these overcomers are the matured sons of God.

The Sons of God

What is the world waiting for? If you read Romans 8 from verse 18 on, you find the whole earth, the whole creation is groaning. Can you hear the groaning of the trees, the groaning of the earth, the groaning of the mountains, volcanoes, the groaning of the waters? The whole creation is groaning because they are under corruption. Who put them there? Man. It is because of the fall of man. God has committed the whole earth to man and man fell, and with the fall of man, the whole creation fell into corruption. They are not willing; they are groaning. What are they waiting for? They are waiting for the manifestation of the sons of God. In other words, not just children, lots of babies, but grown-up sons bearing the character of Christ who can bear responsibility in the house of God. The world is waiting for such people. When this people is fulfilled, manifested, then the whole creation will be delivered from corruption.

The Manchild

You find the same thing in Revelation 12 with the manchild. The manchild is a collective symbol of the overcomers at the last age. When they are matured, when they are born, they will be raptured to the throne of God, and there will be war in the air. Michael and his angels will fight against Satan and his angels, and there will be no more place in the air for Satan. He will be thrown upon this earth. The air is clear for our Lord to descend from the throne to the air.

Who brings in the kingdom? Of course, it is the Lord, but it is the Lord with His church. And then you find judgment will come upon this earth, and the Lord will come down and He will establish His kingdom on this earth. All the kingdoms of this world will eventually become the kingdom of our Lord and of His Christ. Glory, glory to God!

Shall we pray:

Dear Lord, we do sense that we are standing on the verge of a great change. We pray that Thou wilt prepare us for that day. Oh, that we may be those whom Thou can use to bring in Thy kingdom. By Thy grace enable us to overcome even here on this earth, and may our testimony be strong enough to bring down the kingdom of this world and bring in Thy kingdom. We are looking forward to it. In Thy precious name we pray. Amen.

THE KINGDOM AND THE CHRISTIAN

II Peter 1:3-11—As his divine power has given to us all things which relate to life and godliness, through the knowledge of him that has called us by glory and virtue, through which he has given to us the greatest and precious promises, that through these ye may become partakers of the divine nature, having escaped the corruption that is in the world through lust.

But for this very reason also, using therewith all diligence, in your faith have also virtue, in virtue knowledge, in knowledge temperance, in temperance endurance, in endurance godliness, in godliness brotherly love, in brotherly love love: for these things existing and abounding in you make you to be neither idle nor unfruitful as regards the knowledge of our Lord Jesus Christ; for he with whom these things are not present is blind, shortsighted, and has forgotten the purging of his former sins. Wherefore the rather, brethren, use diligence to make your calling and election sure, for doing these things ye will never fall; for thus shall the entrance into the everlasting kingdom of our Lord and Saviour Jesus Christ be richly furnished unto you.

I Corinthians 3:11-15—For other foundation can no man lay besides that which is laid, which is Jesus Christ. Now if any one build upon this foundation, gold, silver, precious stones, wood, grass, straw, the work of each shall be made manifest; for the day shall declare it, because it is revealed in fire; and the fire shall try the work of each what it is. If the work of any one which he has built upon the foundation shall abide, he shall receive a reward. If the work of any one shall be consumed, he shall suffer loss, but he shall be saved, but so as through the fire.

Shall we pray:

Dear Lord, we want to thank You for being with us these days. We thank You because You are not only the beginning, You are also the end. So Lord, as Thou has brought us to the last morning of this conference we look to Thee for the end. Thou art the end of all things because all things are from Thee, through Thee, and unto Thee, and be glory unto Thee. Lord, we just pray that Thou will continue to open Thy Word to our hearts. Speak to us and bring us to where Thou has designed for us. We ask in Thy precious name. Amen.

We thank God for gathering us these days for His Word and for fellowship. And we thank God for being so faithful to us. Everything comes from Him and everything is returned to Him. We have considered together on this matter of the kingdom. When our Lord Jesus was on earth, that is the message He preached. Even after His resurrection, before His ascension, during those forty days when He appeared to His disciples, He still spoke on the kingdom of God. And this is the message our Lord Jesus committed to the church.

From the very beginning of church history, we find the message of the gospel of Jesus Christ that they preached is the gospel of the kingdom. In other words, the emphasis is always on the kingdom. Our Lord Jesus was slain, and God raised Him up, seated Him at the right hand of God, and anointed Him to be the Christ and Lord. God has appointed Him to be the Judge of all the nations. Even at the end of the book of Acts, which of course we know has no end, we find the apostle Paul was still preaching the gospel of the kingdom of God and teaching the things about our Lord Jesus. Unfortunately, today it seems as if the church has forgotten this message. I believe we find the church in its present situation because the gospel of the King, the gospel of the kingdom has not been preached. So by the grace of God, this is something we have been considering together, and hopefully it may really impress upon our hearts.

The gospel of the kingdom of the heavens is not just a theory. It is a truth, and if we know the truth, the truth will set us free. So we look to the Lord that this truth of the gospel of the kingdom of the heavens will be really deeply inscribed upon our hearts and set us free that we may be living literally, spiritually, every day in that kingdom. And then we will look forward to the coming, the returning of our King.

From eternity to eternity our God is God, therefore His kingdom knows no end. His dominion is over all generations. Everything is under His rule and everything expresses His

Kingship, that is, His character. That is the kingdom of God. But as we have mentioned, unfortunately there were rebellions, not only of the angels, but even of man. So strictly speaking, the kingdom of God is where God really rules over a people who listen to Him, who obey Him. That is the reality of the kingdom of God throughout the centuries. Even though His kingdom is over everything, over Satan, over the world, over man, those who are really representing His kingdom are those who submit themselves to the authority, the rule of God, and allow God to work out in their lives His own character that they may be like Him.

We also mentioned the term the kingdom of the heavens. That is the literal translation—the kingdom of the heavens. This special term refers especially to one section in the kingdom of God. It begins with the first coming of our Lord Jesus. The King of the heavens has come to this earth, so that begins the kingdom of the heavens. While He was on earth, He was the King; He was born to be King. And He came to this earth to bring heaven upon earth, the rule of heaven upon earth. But in the beginning the message was:

"The kingdom of the heavens has drawn nigh." Even though He was already here He still said, "The kingdom of the heavens has drawn nigh." Why? It is because He did not have a people to rule over, to enable Him to impart to them His life and to be partakers of His divine nature. But those days were very short because very soon our Lord Jesus said, "The kingdom of the heavens is to be taken by violence and the violent seize on it." In other words, our Lord Jesus began to have His disciples, those who are under His teaching, under His training, under His discipline, and these become the kingdom of the heavens on earth in spiritual reality.

So from that time onward until today, the kingdom of the heavens is now here in the hearts of those who not only believe in the Lord Jesus but also obey Him, trust Him, commit themselves to Him, and allow Him to work out His character in their lives, so that they will be like Him, representing Him on this earth. That is the kingdom of the heavens now. But of course, we know we are looking forward to the day when the kingdom of the heavens shall be publicly manifested on this earth. That will come at the second coming of our Lord Jesus. That is the day we are waiting for, when He shall reign over this earth. The kingdom of this world will become the kingdom of His Lord and of His Christ. Now thank the Lord it is coming.

Then we considered together on this matter of the relationship between the kingdom and the church. The kingdom builds the church. Our Lord Jesus said, "I will build My church." He is the builder but why is it that the building is still unfinished? It is not because the builder is unskillful or is unable to finish. It is because He does not build with dead stones. He is building with living stones such as we are, and we are the problem. He will not do anything against our will. He respects our will. Isn't that tremendous, that God respects our will! He will not force us. Even when we rebel against Him and will not listen to Him, He will persuade, He will beseech. And even as in Romans 12, through His apostle, He will beg. But He will not work without our will, our willing to be His people. So that is the reason why the work is delayed. But thank God, He will finish what He has begun. Our God never leaves anything unfinished. It may take a longer time, but eventually He will finish it.

It is the kingdom that builds the church. We need to submit ourselves to the authority of our King. We need to present our bodies a living sacrifice, not in a sense of working for Him, that will follow, but in the sense of allowing Him to work in us. There is so much in us that is unfit for the kingdom of the heavens, and all these things have to be dealt with. The only material that can be built into the kingdom of the heavens is His life, and His life has to grow in us. We grow up individually and we grow up together, and that can only be done when we are under the headship of Christ. If we continue to be our own heads this work will be delayed. But if we are willing to bow before Him and take Him as our head, our King, obey Him, follow Him in all things, then the work will speed up and it will be done. So this is what authority means. There is no authority except God. Do not think that any one of us has authority in ourselves. We do not have it. Our duty is to submit, to obey. God is the only authority. He may delegate His authority to man, but that delegation is not according to position; that delegation is according to His life. In other words, it is the life of Christ in us that is authority. Other than that, there is no authority.

Our concept of authority is so foreign to God because our concept of authority is the concept of this world. Even in the mind of the disciples, who were with our Lord Jesus in those days, was the thought that authority means to take the highest position, to sit on the right hand and the left hand of our Lord Jesus. Then you are in authority, then you can command, and everybody will have to yield to you. Oh, how we long for that authority! The twelve disciples were always striving and struggling among themselves as to who was the greatest; and we are no different. But our Lord Jesus said, "In the kingdom of this world, that is what authority is. You exercise authority over people and people have to obey you. Not so in the kingdom of the heavens. If you want to be the first, be the last. If you want to be the head, be the bondman of all." This is the way that God exercises His authority. He exercises His authority in love. He exercises His authority in humbling Himself, emptying Himself to become lower and lower. Our Lord

Jesus said, "I am the One who serves, not the One who is served." That is authority.

Authority is life. Authority is love. Authority is sacrifice. Authority is service. It is not taking the high position and commanding other people. With this authority of life in us we minister; we serve one another. And that is the way the church is to be built. And thank God, the church is also the instrument used by God to bring in the kingdom. The whole creation is groaning. They are under corruption unwillingly. They are crying out for liberty, but when will that come? When will all creation be restored to God's original design? Not until the manifestation of the sons of God. So we have a tremendous responsibility.

Now we want to consider together on this matter of the kingdom and you, the kingdom and me. In other words, we do not want to be just talking about the kingdom. We want to make it personal, make it practical. What does the kingdom of the heavens mean to you and to me? What is our attitude towards it? How do we respond to the truth of the kingdom of the heavens? Will our response determine our future, our destiny? These questions are very personal and very important to us.

THE DIFFERENCE BETWEEN GIFT AND REWARD

Before we can answer these questions, probably there is something that we have to understand, and that is the difference between gift and reward. In the mind of many Christians there is only gift; grace, all is grace. Now thank God, God is the giver of all things, that is true. But this matter of reward is almost foreign. The Bible says, "God is the rewarder of those who seek after Him." So God is not only a giver; He is also a rewarder.

What is the difference between gift and reward? Gift depends wholly on the giver. There is no condition upon the receiver. It all depends upon the pleasure of the giver. If He wants to give, He gives, and we just receive it with thankfulness. Reward involves both. It involves the one who works for that reward, and also it depends on the one who gives, the one who dispenses the reward. Gift is free. There is no condition, no discrimination; it is free for all who are willing to receive. But reward is given only to those who are worthy. Gift is pure grace, the grace of God. Reward is work. You have to work to receive a reward. If you do not work, fulfill the conditions, you are not rewarded. So these are two things you find in the Word of God.

The Word of God tells us that God is a great giver. He is the giver of all good things. He loves to give. There is no condition. It is free for all, open. If anyone wills let him come and drink of the river of life. That is grace. But in the Bible you do see this matter of reward. You have to work for it. If you do not, you lose it.

THE KINGDOM: GIFT OR REWARD?

So, is the kingdom a gift or a reward? If the kingdom is a gift, then all you need to do is receive it by faith and all is yours. The way you live the rest of your life has nothing to do with it because it is a gift, a free gift of God. But if it is a reward then if you do not work for it, you will lose it. Now what is it? Thank God, the kingdom is both a gift and a reward. Initially, it is a gift; potentially, it is a gift; positionally, it is a gift.

You remember our Lord Jesus said, "Fear not, little flock, for it is the good pleasure of the Father to give you the kingdom." The kingdom is given, and it is according to the good pleasure of the Father. Therefore do not be afraid; it is yours. But strangely, in the same breath our Lord said, "Seek ye first the kingdom of God and His righteousness, and all these things shall be added unto you." Seek; work for it.

Colossians 1 tells us that by His grace He has delivered us out of the power of darkness and has translated us into the kingdom of the Son of His love. So you are there; you have not done anything. How are you delivered from the power of darkness? You have not done anything. You are under that power. But there is one more powerful than darkness, than the one who holds darkness and He delivers you out of it. That is grace. And He brought you into His own kingdom. So the kingdom is basically, primarily a gift. It is grace. We do not deserve it. All the potential of inheriting the kingdom has been given to us.

In II Peter 1 we are told that His divine power has given to us all things which relate to life and godliness. It is His divine power, and His divine power is so powerful that He has given to us all things concerning life, that means His divine life, and godliness. Godliness simply means "like God." Not only has He given you His life as a gift, but He has also given to you all things that concern godliness. In other words, that life will develop into "like God"; not in the sense of joining the deity, no, but in the sense of taking upon ourselves His character. It is all given. Not only is that life given, we all know that, but even godliness is given. All the potentials are there. It just needs to be developed, that's all.

It is like the children of Israel. God delivered them out of Egypt but that was not God's purpose. God's purpose was to bring them into the Promised Land, flowing with milk and honey. That was the purpose of God. God had already given that land to them. It was theirs. Not only that, but God had already brought them to the border of it and He had all power to bring them into the Promised Land. All the potentials were there, but they needed to go in, put their feet down, and whatever they trod upon was theirs.

In other words, it is a gift, but with the gift it becomes a reward. You have to work for it. Now the two tribes did not want to go into the land. They were satisfied with the land on the east side of the Jordan River. Why? Because they had many cattle. They would rather stay with the cattle and be satisfied than to go into the fulness of God's purpose. How many Christians there are today like that! All has been given. All the provisions have been given. Thank God, He never gives an order or command without first providing and supplying the power to fulfill it.

So the kingdom is a gift but it is also a reward. Even though it is a reward it is still a gift because it is grace. In our mind we think grace and work are contradictory; gift and reward are opposite. But in the Word of God you find that gift and reward, grace and work are complementary. God first worked in; not only the willing but the working, and then we work out our salvation with fear and trembling. So, after all it is grace. We have nothing to boast of.

The only difference is that some people abuse the grace of God or bury the grace of God. But other people respond to grace; they use grace. It is from grace to grace. That is the difference.

In II Peter, everything has been given concerning life and godliness, and He has given us many precious promises to encourage us. It is all through the living knowledge of our Lord Jesus Christ that we may be partakers of His divine nature.

Immediately following that, he said, "For this very reason . . ." because it is such a gift, it is such a provision, "therefore use diligence to make your calling and election sure." If you do not use diligence, then you are blind, you forget your sins have been forgiven, and what grace has been given to you. But if you are diligently seeking, then the result is you will enter into the everlasting kingdom of our Lord Jesus Christ abundantly. That is what God wants us to do. So take courage knowing that after all it is not our doing; it is His working, but He works in us. We must learn to cooperate, to submit ourselves, to allow Him to take charge over us, over our lives. Then He will work out the full salvation.

The kingdom is coming very soon. When Miss Margaret Barber was on earth, one day at the end of the year, brother Watchman Nee and Miss Barber were praying together. This sister was waiting for the Lord's coming, and she told brother Nee, "Maybe when you turn the corner of the street, you will meet Him."

Our Lord is coming. His kingdom is coming to be set up on this earth. Are we waiting for it? Are we longing for it? Are we praying for it? Are we cooperating with it? Today, if we live in the reality of the kingdom of the heavens, when that kingdom comes, you will be there. But if not, you will not be there. Today determines your future destiny.

THE BUILDING MATERIAL

You remember in I Corinthians 3 the apostle Paul said that the foundation is laid and there is no other foundation but Jesus Christ. We are building on Him; we are the extension, as it were, of our Lord Jesus. But the apostle warns us to be careful how we build, what materials we work with. We can build with gold, silver, and precious stones, or we can build with wood, grass, and straw. Gold—the nature of God; silver—the redemption of Christ; precious stone—the work of the Holy Spirit. If our lives and our labor are according to God, out of Christ, in the power of the Holy Spirit, that is the way we build.

Or we can build with wood, grass, and straw. Wood—the nature of man; grass—the beauty of man; straw—the work of man. If we still live according to our old nature, according to the flesh, using our natural strength to build, there are differences. Today, those who build with wood, grass, and straw build very quickly and they can build very huge buildings with almost no cost or little cost. It will be seen; it may be admired and praised today, but one day the fire shall appear. If you build with gold, silver, and precious stone, it costs everything. It costs your life, your self-life, and you cannot build very big. People may not even notice it or see it, but the difference is that one day our work will be tested. Fire will appear.

THE JUDGMENT SEAT OF CHRIST

We do thank God that our Lord Jesus took our judgment upon Himself on Calvary's cross, and because He was judged in our stead we will not be judged before the great white throne. We will not be judged for eternal life or eternal death. That judicial judgment is passed. Thank God for that! But that does not mean as Christians, as the family of God, as in the kingdom of the heavens, that there will be no more judgment. The Bible tells us that one day at His coming we shall all stand before the judgment seat of Christ. In II Corinthians 5:10 it says, "We shall all appear before the judgment seat of Christ, and we will be judged according to our works."

Romans 14:10 tells us: "We shall all appear before the judgment seat of God." It is a time of reckoning from the day you believe in the Lord Jesus, reckoning from the day you come into the family of God, reckoning from the day you are transferred into the kingdom of the Son of His love. How do we live? How do we work? All these things will be judged. It is the judgment seat of Christ, not a throne which is judicial—life and death—but a seat which is family. It is family judgment, to be rewarded or to suffer loss. And this is the fire. Our Lord is a consuming fire. He will judge us according to Himself, judge us according to Christ, how much He has given to us, how much He has revealed to us. To those who receive much, He requires much. We will be judged. If it is wood, grass, straw, it is just the material for the fire and it will be burned up, consumed. In other words, with all that God has so graciously given, with all the potential and the provisions that God has already given you to fulfill, if you still live on your own without submitting yourself to the Lord, all these years are loss. That does not mean you are not saved. It says you are saved. You are still saved, but barely saved.

On the other hand, if you build with gold, silver, and precious stone, it may cost you dearly today, but thank God, when the fire tests you it glows with glory. In other words, you will enter into the kingdom of the heavens and reign with Christ for a thousand years because you are fit for it.

REWARDS

The Bible uses different ways to tell us what the reward will be. Now it is true, even today if you follow the Lord, on one side you seem to lose a lot, but on the other side you are rewarded by the smiling face of our Lord Jesus. You are rewarded with a peace and a joy in the Holy Spirit. You are rewarded by the Lord Himself being with you. But the reward that the Bible especially emphasizes is in the coming kingdom. All the promises, the rewards our Lord Jesus promised to the seven churches, basically, primarily, fully, are all fulfilled in the thousand years.

Our God uses various ways to attract us. "Crown of glory." If we are faithful in what God has committed to us, we will receive the crown of glory.

"Crown of righteousness." If we look forward, waiting for His return, finishing our course, fighting the good fight, keeping the faith, then we will be crowned with a crown of righteousness.

Or we will be crowned with a "Crown of life." If today we suffer, endure sufferings, tribulations for Christ sake, if we endure temptations and overcome them, we will receive the crown of life. If we finish our race we will receive an incorruptible crown.

Sometimes the Bible uses throne—sitting in the throne with our Lord Jesus as He sits with His Father in the throne. Or sometimes it is said there will be five cities, ten cities over which to rule and reign for the Lord according to Him. And sometimes He says, "Come and enter the joy of the Lord," being invited and attending the marriage feast of the Lamb.

Our Lord Jesus tries to encourage us. He knows today we have to deny ourselves, take up the cross, and follow Him, so He encourages us. He said, "There is something waiting there." Some people say, "If you work just for reward that is selfish." So they say, "We do not want any reward; we just love the Lord." That sounds very spiritual. It is true, if your eyes are on the reward only, that is wrong, but to despise what the Lord is pleased to give you is wrong too. We need to seek to be rewarded because it pleases Him. That is the way He wants to do. After all, it is His doing. We have not done anything. We just receive His grace and allow His grace to work through us. That is all. But it pleases Him to reward us as if we have done it. Now isn't that wonderful! Isn't our God so gracious, so loving, so kind, so generous?

Thank God, we have a blessed hope. What are we waiting for? The world is not our home; we are passing through it. And thank God, He is coming. Therefore, the Spirit and the bride say, "Come, Lord Jesus." And may we respond and say, "Come quickly." Thank God He said, "I come."

Let us pray:

Dear Lord, indeed, even though we have not seen Thee, we love Thee; we believe in Thee. But we do look forward to the day when we shall see Thee face to face. Our prayer is that when we see Thee, we will not be put to shame but we will gladden Thy heart. Thank God, You have called us, and You have supplied our every need. Now Lord, may Thy Spirit work it out in each and every one of us, that there will be no regret but only praise and worship. In Thy precious name. Amen.

Other Books Printed By
Christian Testimony Ministry

Speaker	Title
Dana Congdon	Marriage, Singleness, and the Will of God
	Recovery & Restoration
	The Holy Spirit
	Hebrews
A.J. Flack	Tent of His Splendour
Stephen Kaung	Acts
	Be Ye Therefore Perfect
	Called Out Unto Christ
	Called to the Fellowship of God's Son
	Divine Life and Order
	For Me to Live is Christ
	Glorious Liberty of the Children of God
	God's Purpose for the Family
	I Will Build My Church
	Meditations on the Kingdom
	Recovery
	Spiritual Exercise
	Spiritual Life (II Corinthians Series)
	Teach Us to Pray
	The Cross
	The Fulness of Christ—In the Book of Revelation
	The Headship of Christ
	The Kingdom and the Church
	The Kingdom of God
	The Last Call to the Churches, the Call to Overcome
	The Life of Our Lord Jesus
	The Life of the Church, the Body of Christ
	The Lord's Table
	Two Guideposts for Inheriting the Kingdom
	Vision of Christ (Revelation)
	Who Are We?

WHY DO WE SO GATHER?
WORSHIP

LANCE LAMBERT

CALLED UNTO HIS ETERNAL GLORY
GOD'S ETERNAL PURPOSE
IN THE DAY OF THY POWER
JACOB I HAVE LOVED
LIVING FAITH
LESSONS FROM THE LIFE OF MOSES
LOVE DIVINE
MY HOUSE SHALL BE A HOUSE OF PRAYER
PREPARATION FOR THE COMING OF THE LORD
REIGNING WITH CHRIST
SPIRITUAL CHARACTER
THE GOSPEL OF THE KINGDOM
THE IMPORTANCE OF COVERING
THE LAST DAYS AND GOD'S PRIORITIES
THE PRIZE
THE SUPREMACY OF JESUS CHRIST
THINE IS THE POWER!
THOU ART MINE

T. AUSTIN-SPARKS

THE LORD'S TESTIMONY AND THE WORLD NEED

HARVEY CEDARS CONFERENCE

STEPHEN KAUNG

HEAVENLY VISION
SPIRITUAL RESPONSIBILITY

CONGDON, HILE, KAUNG

SPIRITUAL MINISTRY
SPIRITUAL AUTHORITY
SPIRITUAL HOUSE
SPIRITUAL SUBMISSION

STEPHEN KAUNG

SPIRITUAL KNOWLEDGE
SPIRITUAL POWER
SPIRITUAL REALITY
SPIRITUAL VALUE
SPIRITUAL BLESSING
SPIRITUAL DISCERNMENT

www.ingramcontent.com/pod-product-compliance
Lightning Source LLC
Chambersburg PA
CBHW061738020426
42331CB00006B/1278